BIG PICTURE 📷 SPORTS

Meet the
INDIANAPOLIS
COLTS

By
ZACK BURGESS

NORWOOD HOUSE 🏠 PRESS

CHICAGO, ILLINOIS

NorwoodHouse Press

P.O. Box 316598 • Chicago, Illinois 60631
For more information about Norwood House Press please visit our website at
www.norwoodhousepress.com or call 866-565-2900.

Photo Credits:
All photos courtesy of Associated Press, except for the following: TCMA, Inc. (6),
Topps, Inc. (10 top, 11 bottom), Philadelphia Chewing Gum Co. (10 bottom, 11 top),
The Upper Deck Co. (11 middle), Black Book Archives (15, 18, 22), Fleer Corp. (23).

Cover Photo: Todd Rosenberg/Associated Press

The football memorabilia photographed for this book is part of the authors' collection. The collectibles used
for artistic background purposes in this series were manufactured by many different card companies—
including Bowman, Donruss, Fleer, Leaf, O-Pee-Chee, Pacific, Panini America, Philadelphia Chewing Gum,
Pinnacle, Pro Line, Pro Set, Score, Topps, and Upper Deck—as well as several food brands, including
Crane's, Hostess, Kellogg's, McDonald's and Post.

Designer: Ron Jaffe
Series Editors: Mike Kennedy and Mark Stewart
Project Management: Black Book Partners, LLC.
Editorial Production: Lisa Walsh

Library of Congress Cataloging-in-Publication Data
Names: Burgess, Zack.
Title: Meet the Indianapolis Colts / by Zack Burgess.
Description: Chicago, Illinois : Norwood House Press, [2016] | Series: Big
picture sports | Includes bibliographical references and index. |
Audience: Grade: K to Grade 3.
Identifiers: LCCN 2015026326| ISBN 9781599537313 (Library Edition : alk.
paper) | ISBN 9781603578349 (eBook)
Subjects: LCSH: Indianapolis Colts (Football team)--Miscellanea--Juvenile
literature.
Classification: LCC GV956.I53 B87 2016 | DDC 796.332/640977252--dc23
LC record available at http://lccn.loc.gov/2015026326

288N—072016
Manufactured in the United States of America in North Mankato, Minnesota

CONTENTS

Words in **bold type** are defined on page 24.

The Colts celebrate another amazing play.

CALL ME A COLT

Colts are young horses full of surprises. The Indianapolis Colts always try to live up to their name. They use power and speed to win games. Their fans never know what to expect from them next. At any moment, the Colts might do something amazing.

TIME MACHINE

The Colts played their first season in the National Football League (NFL) in 1953. Maryland was their home for 31 years. In 1984, the Colts moved to Indiana. They have always relied on great quarterbacks. Their three best were **Johnny Unitas**, Peyton Manning, and Andrew Luck.

Andrew Luck looks for an open receiver.

The roof is open at the Colts' stadium.

Best Seat in the House

The Colts' stadium is one of the most modern in football. The roof can open and close. That means the fans are comfortable in any kind of weather. The stadium also offers great views of the Indianapolis skyline.

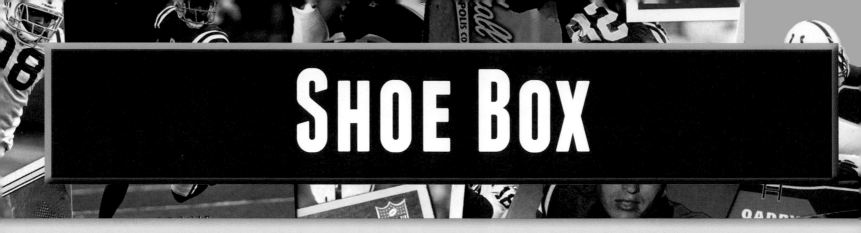

SHOE BOX

The trading cards on these pages show some of the best Colts ever.

JOHNNY UNITAS

QUARTERBACK · 1956-1972

Johnny was known as "The Golden Arm." He was a master at moving the Colts down the field with the game on the line.

LENNY MOORE
BALTIMORE COLTS   HALFBACK

LENNY MOORE

RUNNING BACK · 1956-1967

Lenny was a great runner and pass-catcher. He once scored a touchdown in 18 games in a row.

BOB BOYD

CORNERBACK · 1960-1968

Bob was a quarterback in college. His knowledge of the passing game made him a great defensive player.

MARVIN HARRISON

RECEIVER · 1996-2008

Marvin was Peyton Manning's favorite target. He set an NFL record with 143 catches in 2002.

ANDREW LUCK

QUARTERBACK · FIRST YEAR WITH TEAM: 2012

Andrew was a great leader. The Colts went to the **playoffs** in each of his first three seasons.

THE BIG PICTURE

Look at the two photos on page 13. Both appear to be the same. But they are not. There are three differences. Can you spot them?

Answers on page 23.

TRUE OR FALSE?

Peyton Manning was a star quarterback. Two of these facts about him are **TRUE**. One is **FALSE**. Do you know which is which?

 1 Peyton was the NFL's Most Valuable Player four times from 2003 to 2009.

 2 Peyton once booted a field goal when the Colts' kicker was injured.

 3 Peyton was voted **All-Pro** five times for the Colts.

Answer on page 23.

Peyton Manning was one of the best passers in team history.

Colts fans are crazy about their team.

Go Colts, Go!

Colts fans are famous for their love and knowledge of their team. Before games, they tailgate in the stadium parking lot. They do this on sunny fall days and on snowy winter days. Nothing stops them from supporting their Colts.

ON THE MAP

Here is a look at where five Colts were born, along with a fun fact about each.

1 **DUANE BICKETT · LOS ANGELES, CALIFORNIA**
Duane was the Colts' first pick in the 1985 NFL **draft**.

2 **REGGIE WAYNE · NEW ORLEANS, LOUISIANA**
Reggie led the NFL with 1,510 receiving yards in 2007.

3 **DWIGHT FREENEY · HARTFORD, CONNECTICUT**
Dwight made the **Pro Bowl** seven times as a Colt.

4 **EDGERRIN JAMES · IMMOKALEE, FLORIDA**
Edgerrin led the NFL in rushing yards in his first two seasons.

5 **TED HENDRICKS · GUATEMALA CITY, GUATEMALA**
Ted was a defensive leader on the Colts' 1970 Super Bowl team.

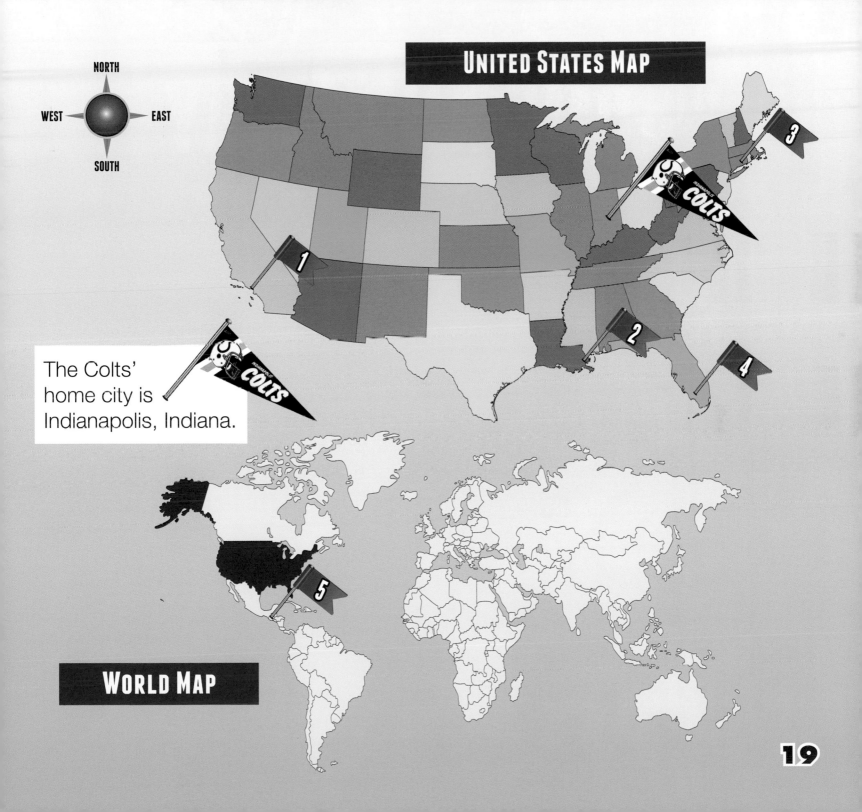

NORTH

WEST   EAST

SOUTH

The Colts' home city is Indianapolis, Indiana.

1

2

3

4

5

WORLD MAP

19

Home and Away

D'Qwell Jackson wears the Colts' home uniform.

Football teams wear different uniforms for home and away games. The main colors of the Colts have been blue and white for more than 60 seasons.

T.Y. Hilton wears the Colts' away uniform.

The Colts' helmet is one of the most famous in the NFL. It is white with a blue horseshoe on each side. The team has used this design since the 1950s.

WE WON!

In the years before the Super Bowl, the Colts won the NFL championship twice, in 1958 and 1959. They have also won the Super Bowl twice. Their first victory came in 1970. Their next Super Bowl win came in 2006 under coach **Tony Dungy**.

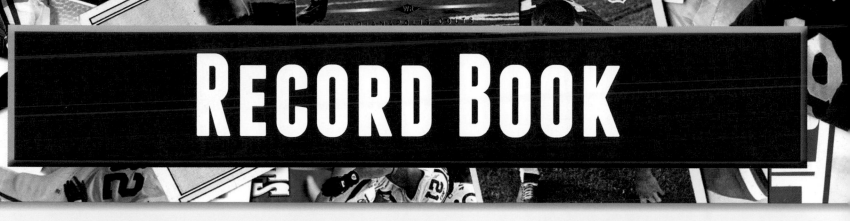

RECORD BOOK

These Colts set team records.

PASSING YARDS	RECORD
Season: Andrew Luck (2014)	4,761
Career: Peyton Manning	54,828

TOUCHDOWN CATCHES	RECORD
Season: Marvin Harrison (2001 & 2004)	15
Career: Marvin Harrison	128

RUSHING TOUCHDOWNS	RECORD
Season: Lenny Moore (1964)	16
Career: **Edgerrin James**	64

ANSWERS FOR THE BIG PICTURE
#60 changed to #09 on his shoulder, the horseshoe on #74's helmet turned upside down, and #36's socks changed to light blue.

ANSWER FOR TRUE AND FALSE
#2 is false. Peyton never booted a field goal for the Colts.

23

FOOTBALL WORDS

INDEX

All-Pro
An honor given to the best NFL player at each position.

Draft
The meeting each spring when NFL teams select the top college players.

Playoffs
The games played after the regular season that decide which teams will play in the Super Bowl.

Pro Bowl
The NFL's annual all-star game.

Photos are on **BOLD** numbered pages.

ABOUT THE AUTHOR

Zack Burgess has been writing about sports for more than 20 years. He has lived all over the country and interviewed lots of All-Pro football players, including Brett Favre, Eddie George, Jerome Bettis, Shannon Sharpe, and Rich Gannon. Zack was the first African American beat writer to cover Major League Baseball when he worked for the *Kansas City Star*.

ABOUT THE COLTS

Learn more at these websites:
www.colts.com • www.profootballhof.com
www.teamspiritextras.com/Overtime/html/colts.html